SMALL ROOMS FOR KIDS
PETITES CHAMBRES D'ENFANT
KLEINE KINDERZIMMER

SMALL ROOMS FOR KIDS
PETITES CHAMBRES D'ENFANT
KLEINE KINDERZIMMER

EVERGREEN

EVERGREEN is an imprint of

Taschen GmbH

© 2006 TASCHEN GmbH

Hohenzollernring 53, D-50672 Köln

www.taschen.com

Editor Éditrice Redakteur:
Simone Schleifer

English translation Traduction anglaise Englische Übersetzung:
Heather Bagott

French translation Traduction française Französische Übersetzung:
Marion Westerhoff

Proofreading Relecture Korrektur lesen:
Matthew Clarke, Lou Andrea Savoir, Anja Llorella Oriol

Art director Direction artistique Art Direktor:
Mireia Casanovas Soley

Graphic design and layout Mise en page et maquette Graphische Gestaltung und Layout:
Elisabet Rodríguez Lázaro

Printed by Imprimé par Gedruckt durch:
Gráficas Toledo, Spain

ISBN-13: 978-3-8228-2788-8
ISBN-10: 3-8228-2788-6

Children's bedrooms constitute the space where the smallest members of the family grow up and where different phases of their development unfold, a place where they play, learn, sleep and dream. The setting should be attractive and inviting, with a design corresponding to the age of the child.

In fact, every age range is marked by special needs, so the layout of a child's bedroom should be carefully thought out from the start. For example, newborn babies are happiest in a crib or a pram but soon, as their mobility increases, they will need a little bed, a wardrobe and a small table for nappy changing. Thus, the best idea is to choose furniture that "grows with the child" and can be adapted to their needs by changing the existing components or by later buying additional pieces. The layout of the furniture is an important aspect to consider, in order to maximize the space available. So, a small bedroom for children should be easy to alter, with many options, as well as the desired atmosphere.

Also, the choice of colors can enlarge a bedroom visually. For example, colors such as raspberry pink, light blue, lemon yellow and pale green create a cozier atmosphere and give a sense of space that makes a room seem bigger. The color of the toys, accessories and furniture can produce a similar effect. Striking contrasts can be achieved through simple ideas, such as a pink chest filled with soft animal toys or a collection of colorful pictures.

The following pages present ideas of renowned designers, interior architects and manufacturers from all over the world, for babies, small children and teenagers. There are all types of practical solutions in fun colors, brimming with imaginative proposals, which include everything from classic design and informal styles, to the most modern and avant-garde concepts.

La chambre d'enfant est un univers où grandissent les plus jeunes membres de la famille, l'espace dans lequel ils traversent différentes phases de développement. C'est une pièce où jouer, apprendre, dormir et rêver. L'atmosphère ambiante doit être agréable et accueillante, aménagée en fonction de l'âge de l'enfant.

En effet, à chaque tranche d'âge correspondent des besoins particuliers. Par conséquent, l'agencement de la chambre d'enfant doit être, d'emblée, très bien conçu. Dans les premières semaines, le nouveau-né se sentira mieux dans un berceau ou dans un landau. Mais dès ses premiers mouvements, il lui faudra un lit, une armoire et une table à langer. Il est donc judicieux de choisir dès le départ des meubles qui « grandissent avec l'enfant ». Ajouter un élément modulable ou acheter des meubles individuels permet de satisfaire les besoins de l'enfant au fur et à mesure qu'il grandit. De même, il est essentiel d'optimiser l'agencement du mobilier en fonction de l'espace disponible. Pour ce faire, il y a mille et une façons d'aménager judicieusement les petites chambres, en utilisant jusqu'au dernier recoin pour créer l'atmosphère escomptée.

Le bon usage des couleurs permet également d'agrandir visuellement une petite chambre d'enfant. Les tons pastel glacés à l'instar du rose framboise, du bleu ciel, du jaune citron ou du vert pâle accentuent l'impression d'espace. Si les enfants adorent les couleurs intenses et vives, il n'est pas nécessaire d'en badigeonner tous les murs. Jouets, accessoires et meubles l'enfant peuvent produire le même effet : de petites touches de couleur, comme par exemple une boîte rose remplie d'animaux en peluche ou une collection d'images multicolores, peuvent avoir l'effet désiré.

Au fil des pages, cet ouvrage présente des projets adaptés à chaque tranche d'âge, du nouveau-né à l'enfant et l'adolescent, signés par les plus grands designers, architectes d'intérieur et fabricants du monde entier : un éventail de solutions imaginatives, hautes en couleurs, allant d'agencements classiques à des formules plus informelles, des concepts modernes ou carrément avant-gardistes.

Das Kinderzimmer ist der Raum, in dem die kleinsten Familienmitglieder heranwachsen und die unterschiedlichen Phasen ihrer Entwicklung durchleben - ein Raum zum Spielen, Lernen, Schlafen und Träumen. Es sollte daher eine freundliche, einladende und vor allem dem jeweiligen Alter entsprechende Atmosphäre geschaffen werden.

Die Einrichtung des Kinderzimmers sollte von Anfang an gut durchdacht sein, denn naturgemäß ergeben sich für jede Altersstufe besondere Anforderungen. Das Neugeborene beispielsweise fühlt sich in den ersten Wochen in einer Wiege oder einem Stubenwagen am wohlsten, jedoch schon sehr bald – mit zunehmendem Bedürfnis nach Bewegung – braucht es dann ein Bettchen, einen Schrank und eine Wickelkommode. So ist es sinnvoll, sich von vornherein für Kindermöbel zu entscheiden, die "mitwachsen". Sie lassen sich durch Umbau der vorhandenen Teile oder Nachkauf einzelner Möbel den Bedürfnissen des älter werdenden Kindes anpassen. Ein weiterer grund-legender Aspekt hinsichtlich des Mobiliars ist es, bei seiner Anordnung eine maximale Ausnutzung des zur Verfü-gung stehenden Platzes zu erreichen. Hierbei werden bei der Gestaltung kleiner Kinderzimmer eine Vielzahl unter-schiedlicher Möglichkeiten geboten, die es zulassen, den Raumes weitmöglichst auszuschöpfen und dabei die gewünschte Atmosphäre herzustellen.

Auch der Einsatz gezielt ausgewählter Farben ist ein Mittel, um kleine Kinderzimmer optisch größer wirken zu las-sen. So wirken pastellige Eistöne wie Himbeerrosa, Hellblau, Zitronengelb und Blassgrün freundlich, vermitteln den Eindruck von Weite und lassen den Raum größer erscheinen. Kinder lieben zweifellos intensive und leuchten-de Farben, jedoch ist es nicht unbedingt notwendig, die Wände großflächig damit zu streichen. Auch farbige Spiel-sachen, Accessoires und Möbel, die die Kinder umgeben, können eine ebenso wirkungsvolle Ausstrahlung haben. Schon kleine Akzente, wie etwa eine pinkfarbene Box gefüllt mit Stofftierchen oder eine Sammlung von bunten Bildern schaffen lebendige Kontraste.

Auf den folgenden Seiten werden Entwürfe für die unterschiedlichen Altersstufen vom Neugeborenen über das Kleinkind bis hin zum Jugendlichen namenhafter Designer, Innenarchitekten und Fabrikanten aus aller Welt vorge-stellt: phantasievolle, farbenfrohe und praktische Lösungen aller Art, von der klassischen Einrichtung über kokett-verspielte bis hin zu avantgardistisch-modernen Entwürfen.

SMALL ROOMS FOR KIDS
PETITES CHAMBRES D'ENFANT
KLEINE KINDERZIMMER

Design Criteria
Critères de design
Designaspekte

Children's development is greatly influenced by their surroundings. It is therefore important to reach a balance between excessive activity and monotony, in order to allow them to be stimulated but also to rest.
Babies require, above all, a space that provides warmth and security, while older children will increasingly demand a say in the look of their room. This can involve the use of bright colors and amusing accessories like bedcovers and lamps.

L'environnement de l'enfant exerce une influence prépondérante sur son développement. Il est donc important de trouver un équilibre entre stimulation excessive et monotonie, afin d'encourager l'apprentissage autant que le repos.
Bébé, l'enfant à tout d'abord besoin d'un environnement chaleureux et sécurisant. En grandissant, il aura de plus en plus envie de participer à l'agencement de la pièce. L'emploi de couleurs vives ou d'accessoires amusants, comme portemanteaux ou lampes, permet d'aller dans ce sens.

Die räumliche Umgebung eines Kindes beeinflußt seine Entwicklung in grundlegendem Maße. So ist es wichtig eine Balance zwischen Reizüberflutung und Monotonie herzustellen, um dadurch sowohl Stimulation als auch Ruhe zu ermöglichen.
Während im Säuglingsalter der Raum in erster Linie Wärme und Geborgenheit vermitteln soll, wächst mit zunehmendem Alter der Wunsch der Kinder nach Mitgestaltung. Durch Verwendung lebendiger Farben oder auch lustiger Accessoires wie Kleiderhaken oder Beleuchtungskörper kann diesem Bedürfnis Rechnung getragen werden.

Distribution
Distribution
Raumaufteilung

Lighting
Éclairage
Beleuchtung

Materials
Matériaux
Materialien

Colors
Couleurs
Farben

Distribution Distribution Raumaufteilung

An orderly layout makes it possible to offset the untidyness that inevitably reigns in a child's bedroom. Storage systems, such as boxes that fit one on top of the other, chests, and shelves are the most practical means for storing toys in their appropriate place. The furniture layout should guarantee easy access to the toys or equipment for baby care.

Une distribution claire permettra de pallier au désordre qui règne inévitablement dans une chambre d'enfant. Des systèmes de rangement adéquats, à l'instar de caisses superposables, de tiroirs et d'étagères, permettent aux enfants d'ordonner clairement leurs petites affaires afin que chaque chose soit bien à sa place. Un arrangement judicieux du mobilier permet d'atteindre facilement les jouets ou les ustensiles indispensables aux soins du bébé.

Dem Chaos im Kinderzimmer sollte man mit sinnvollen Ordnungssystemen sowie einer klaren Raumaufteilung begegnen. Damit die Kinder ihre Besitztümer leicht verstauen können, sind Aufbewahrungssysteme wie stapelbare Kisten, Schubladen und Regalflächen erforderlich. Zudem wird durch eine zweckmäßige Anordnung des Mobiliars die einfache Erreichbarkeit sowohl der Spielsachen als auch der für die Babypflege erforderlichen Utensilien gewährleistet.

© Tisettanta

© Galli

© Andrea Martiradonna

Lighting Éclairage Beleuchtung

The combination of natural and artificial light guarantees ideal lighting in a child's bedroom. During the day this space generally receives enough daylight to allow its young occupants to play or do their homework in a diaphanous atmosphere. However, at night the light must also be sufficient, albeit softer. Illuminated figures are ideal for this purpose, as well as being attractive decorative features.

L'alliance de lumière naturelle et artificielle permet d'éclairer de manière optimale la chambre d'enfant. Dans la journée, il est indispensable de veiller à ce que la pièce reçoive suffisamment de lumière naturelle, pour que nos petits occupants puissent jouer ou faire leurs devoirs à la lumière du jour. Le soir, l'éclairage, plus tamisé, doit être suffisant. Citons à cet effet les figurines lumineuses qui conjuguent décoration et fonction.

Für eine optimale Beleuchtung im Kinderzimmer sorgt die Kombination aus natürlichem und künstlichem Licht. Tagsüber ist es sinnvoll, den Raum mit viel Tageslicht zu versorgen, so dass die kleinen Bewohner in einer hellen Atmosphäre spielen oder ihre Hausaufgaben absolvieren können. Aber auch abends sollte für eine ausreichende Beleuchtung gesorgt werden. Hier können illuminierte Figuren neben ihrer Funktion gleichzeitig einen dekorativen Zweck erfüllen.

© MyToys/Haba

© MyToys/Haba

Materials Matériaux Materialen

Design, and above all, resistance and durability must be considered when choosing materials for children's bedrooms. Materials such as wood, wicker, plastic or cloth define the image of the room and must provide not only warmth but also safety, by being free of sharp corners or edges and loose pieces. It is also important to choose antiallergic and saliva-resistant materials, varnishes and coverings.

Les matériaux pour la chambre d'enfants doivent prendre en compte, mis à part le design, des critères de solidité et de facilité d'entretien. Bois, osier, plastique et tissus sont des matières qui en plus d'être chaleureuses sont conformes aux normes de sécurité pour enfants – sans arrêtes vives, coins saillants, ni éléments détachables. Un autre critère essentiel dans le choix de matières : laques et revêtements doivent résister à la salive et être antiallergiques.

Bei der Materialwahl im Kinderzimmer sollte neben dem Design vor allem Wert auf Robustheit und Pflegeleichtigkeit gelegt werden. Materialien wie Holz, Korb, Plastik und Stoff vermitteln nicht nur Wärme sondern haben darüber hinaus den Vorteil, Kindersicher zu sein – sprich ohne scharfe Ecken, Kanten oder sich ablösende Teile. Ein weiteres, unverzichtbares Kriterium sollte in der Auswahl speichelfester und allergiegeprüfter Materialen und Beschichtungen liegen.

© Heather Spencer Designs

Plastic
Plastique
Plastik

© Ikea

© Ikea

© Babymobel

31

Painted Wood

Bois peint

Bemaltes Holz

© Heather Spencer Designs

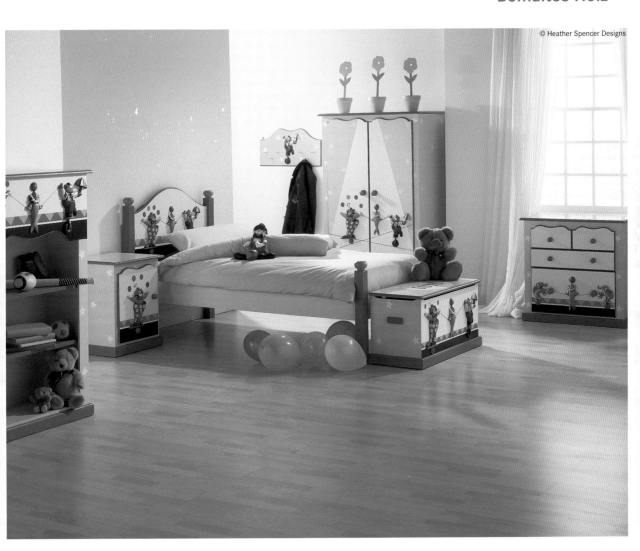

Wicker
Osier
Korbwaren

© Leipold

© Heather Spencer Designs

© Jacadi

© Jacadi

© Jacadi

© Jacadi

Colors Couleurs Farben

When painting a children's bedroom it is important to take into account their imaginatioin and creativity. The larger the space, the more care is needed in the use of colors. The dominant color defines the atmosphere, while the others have a differentiating effect and should harmonize with the main color. The color details will stand out from the background splashes of color and should be used in moderation.

Le choix de la couleur de la chambre d'enfant doit laisser assez de place à son imagination et esprit créatif. Plus l'espace est important, plus il est indispensable de se limiter au niveau des couleurs. Le ton dominant détermine l'atmosphère générale et les autres couleurs servent à apporter du contraste. Celles-ci doivent être en harmonie avec la couleur de base. Les touches de couleur ressortiront beaucoup et de ce fait sont à utiliser avec parcimonie.

Wichtig bei der Farbgebung im Kinderzimmer ist, dem Kind ausreichend Freiraum für Kreativität und Phantasie zu lassen. Je größer eine Fläche ist, desto zurückhaltender sollten Farben verwendet werden. Die quantitativ vorherrschende Farbe gibt die Grundstimmung an, während weitere Farben das Raumbild differenzieren. Farbakzente heben sich gegen die Farbflächen ab und sollten deshalb eher in gesättigten kleinen Proportionen verwendet werden.

Orange

44

Blue
Bleu
Blau

Pink
Rose
Rosa

© Tisettanta

Green

Vert

Grün

© Assomobili

49

Projects
Projets
Projekte

The design and furniture of a child's bedroom largely depends on the age of the child. Whereas a peaceful atmosphere with soft light and a controlled temperature is essential in a baby's room, in a small child's bedroom it is vital to take full advantage of the space to create a play area. A teenager's room, however, requires a layout in order to create a stimulating atmosphere conducive to study. For this reason, the following chapter is structured by age into three sections offering different design solutions.

Le design et l'ameublement de la chambre d'enfant dépendent essentiellement de son âge. Si dans la chambre du nourrisson, il est primordial de créer une atmosphère calme et de régler facilement la température et l'éclairage, dans celle de l'enfant en bas-âge, il est essentiel d'optimiser l'espace disponible pour qu'il puisse jouer. Ensuite l'aménagement de la chambre d'adolescent doit permettre de créer une ambiance de travail et d'apprentissage agréable pour le stimuler et favoriser l'inspiration. Le chapitre suivant est divisé en trois tranches d'âge pour différencier les différentes solutions de design en fonction de ces groupes.

Das Design sowie die Einrichtungsgegenstände des Kinderzimmers sind stark vom Alter der Bewohner abhängig. Während im Zimmer des Säuglings vor allem Wert auf eine ruhige Atmosphäre sowie eine einfache Temperatur- und Lichtregulierung des Raumes gelegt wird, so steht im Kleinkindzimmer eine optimale Ausnutzung des vorhandenen Platzes als Spielfläche im Vordergrund. Bei der Gestaltung des Jugendzimmers wiederum ist es wichtig, eine angenehme Lernatmosphäre herzustellen, um so den Heranwachsenden zu inspieren und animieren. Um die unterschiedlichen Designlösungen für jede Altersgruppe differenziert darzustellen, ist das folgende Kapitel in drei Altersgruppen unterteilt.

Babies
Bébés
Babys

Small Children
Enfants en bas-âge
Kleinkinder

Teenagers
Adolescents
Jugendliche

Babies Bébés Babys

Warm pastel colors, such as light blue, pink, pale green and light yellow are preferable in the design of baby's room. The sensorial perception of a child at this age is in its first stage of development and therefore intense optical stimulation should be avoided. The space should also be as empty as possible to ensure easy maintenance and strict hygiene.

Dans les chambres d'enfant, on privilégie en général les tons pastel, comme le bleu clair, le rose, le vert pâle ou un jaune doux. A cet âge, la perception sensorielle de l'enfant est dans sa première phase de développement. Il est donc conseillé de renoncer à de trop fortes stimulations optiques et de dégager les surfaces au maximum, pour faciliter l'entretien et assurer une hygiène parfaite.

Bei der Gestaltung des Babyzimmers werden bevorzugt warme Pastelltöne wie hellblau, rosa, blassgrün oder ein sanftes Gelb verwendet. Die Sinneswahrnehmung des Kindes ist in diesem Alter in der ersten Entwicklungsphase und so sollte auf zu starke optische Stimulation verzichtet werden. Desweiteren ist es sinnvoll, Flächen möglichst frei zu halten, um absolute Hygiene bei leichter Pflege zu garantieren.

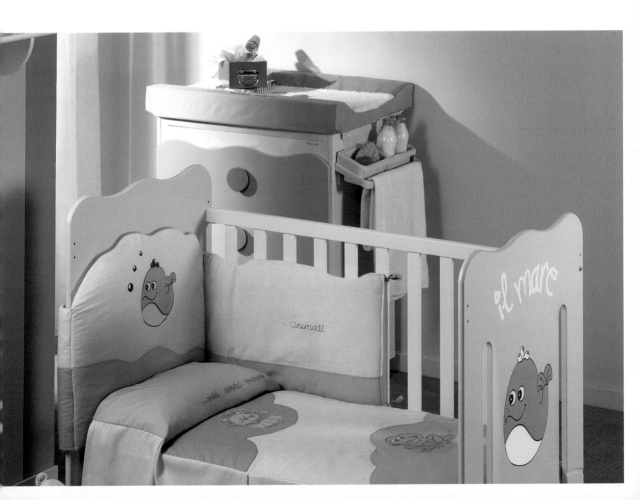

Baby's Paradise
Un paradis pour bébés
Babys Paradies

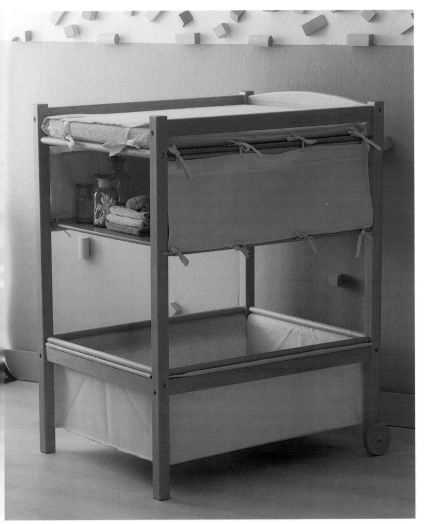

Nature
Nature
Natur

Enric Ruiz & Olga Subirós / Cloud 9

Pastel Colors
Tons pastels
Pastelltöne

Blue Harmony

Harmonie en bleu

Blaue Harmonie

Mònica Pla

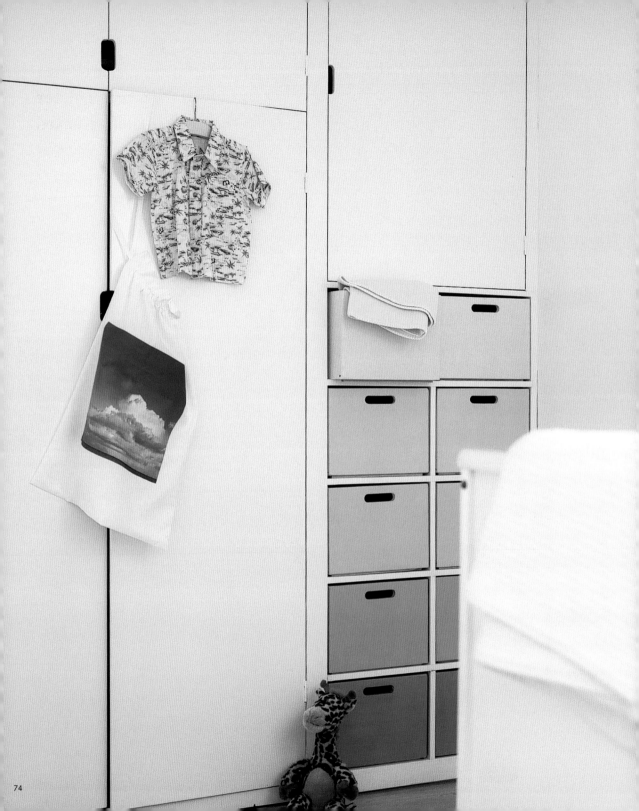

Fun Boxes
Boîtes rigolotes
Lustige Boxen
Homebase

Princess
Princesse
Prinzessin
Micuna

Warm Atmosphere
Ambiance chaleureuse
Warmes Ambiente
Estudio Esténcil

Small Children Enfants en bas-âge Kleinkinder

It is at this age that children develop their sense of independence and initiative by exploring their surroundings through play. It should therefore be a big enough space for them to play without obstacles. Blackboards or drawing surfaces serve to build the child's creativity while also having a decorative function. The chromatic range of a small child's bedroom should be dominated by bold, bright colors.

C'est l'âge où l'enfant, qui développe son sentiment d'indépendance et d'initiative, découvre son environnement de manière ludique. Il lui faut donc suffisamment de place pour jouer sans être dérangé. Tableaux et surfaces aptes à être peintes permettront à l'enfant de développer sa créativité, tout en remplissant leur fonction décorative. Dans la chambre de l'enfant en bas-âge, la palette de couleurs se décline surtout dans des teintes soutenues et gaies.

In diesem Alter wächst das Gefühl von Autonomie und Eigeninitiative und das Kleinkind erkundet seine Umwelt auf spielerische Art und Weise. Somit sollte ausreichend Platz zum ungestörten Spiel vorhanden sein. Auch die Anbringung von Tafeln und bemalbaren Flächen ist eine Möglichkeit die Kreativität des Kindes zu fördern und zugleich eine dekorative Funktion zu erfüllen. Das Farbspektrum im Kleinkinderzimmer wird von kräftigen, frohen Tönen dominiert.

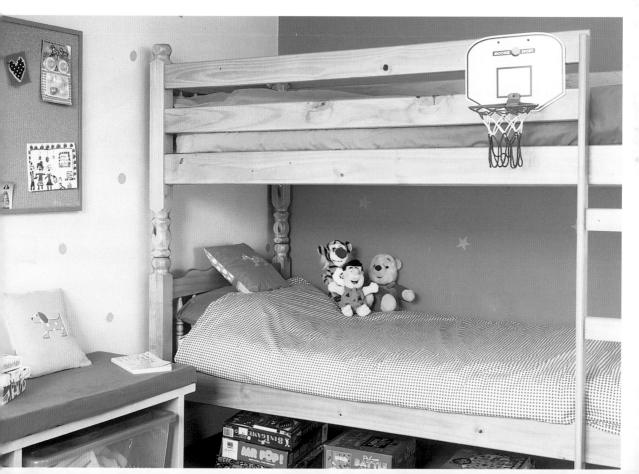

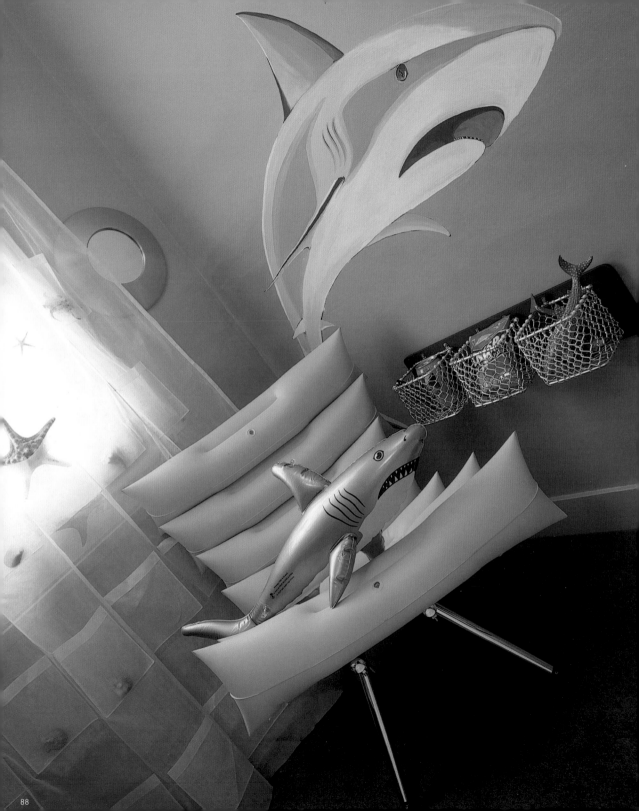

Sharks

Requins

Haie

Jenny Norton/Norton Crane

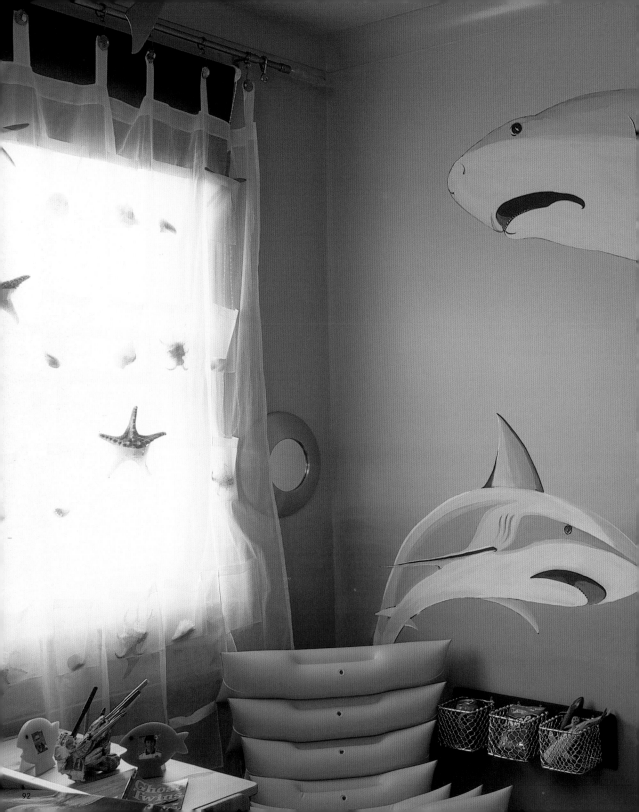

The Ocean
L'océan
Der Ozean
Ikea

Fairy Pink
Rose féerique
Elfenrosa

Jenny Norton/Norton Crane

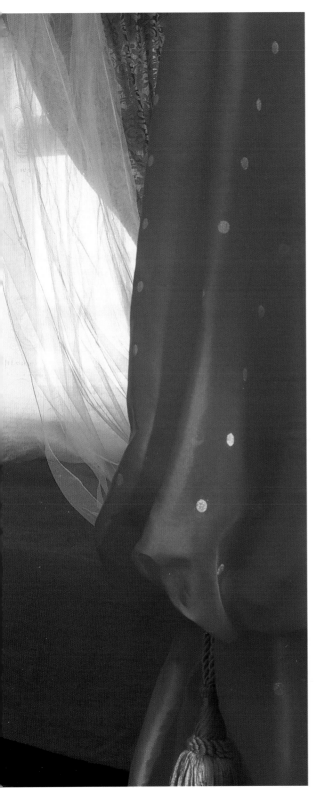

Butterfly Forest
Forêt de papillons
Schmetterlingswald

Jenny Norton / Norton Crane

Purple, Red, Green
Violet, rouge, vert
Lila, Rot, Grün

Colored Circles

Cercles en couleur

Farbige Kreise

Amelia Aran

Orange

Álex Serra

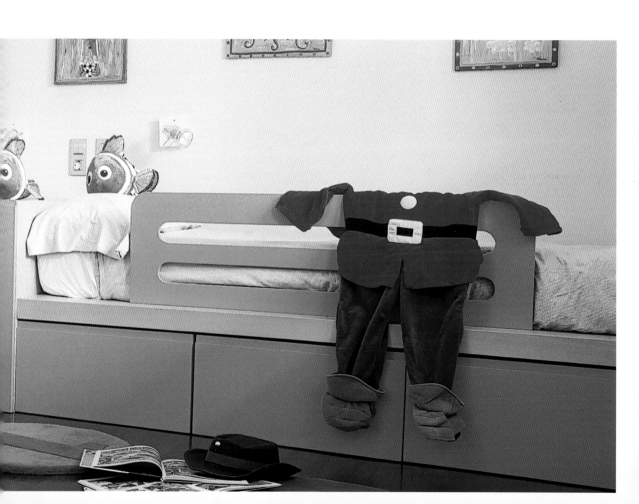

© José Luis Hausmann

Mauve
Mauve
Malve
Ramón Peñarroya

Boy's Room
Chambre de garçon
Jungenzimmer

Deu i Deu Interiorista / Ana Profitós

Teenagers Adolescents Jugendliche

The creation of a personal lifestyle and the search for identity characterize this last phase of infancy. So, young persons need a space which can be organized in harmony with their own ideas. Given that all the activities take place in one space, the aim would be to achieve a rational layout of the furniture. In this way, the desk should take full advantage of the daytime light, while the bed should be located in the darkest part of the room.

Cette dernière étape de l'enfant se définit par le développement du style de vie personnel et la quête de l'identité. Les jeunes ont donc besoin d'un espace qu'ils peuvent agencer à leur goût. Toutes les activités se déroulant dans une pièce unique, on favorisera une distribution judicieuse des meubles. Par exemple, si le bureau doit bénéficier au maximum de la lumière du jour, le lit sera au contraire placé dans le coin le plus sombre de la chambre.

Die Ausbildung des eigenen Lebensstils und die Identitätsfindung kennzeichnen diese letzte Kindheitsphase. Deshalb benötigen Jugendliche einen Raum, der nach eigenen Ideen gestaltet werden kann. Da alle Aktivitäten in einem einzigen Raum stattfinden, liegt das Ziel der Gestaltung darin, eine sinnvolle Anordnung zu finden. So sollte etwa der Schreibtisch maximal vom Tageslicht profitieren, das Bett hingegen im dunkelsten Bereich positioniert werden.

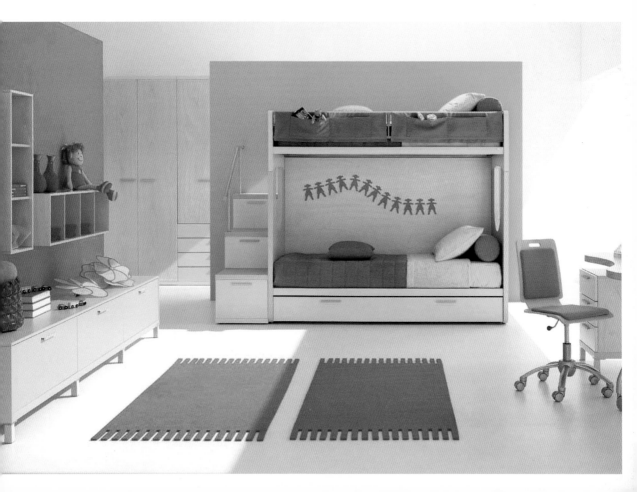

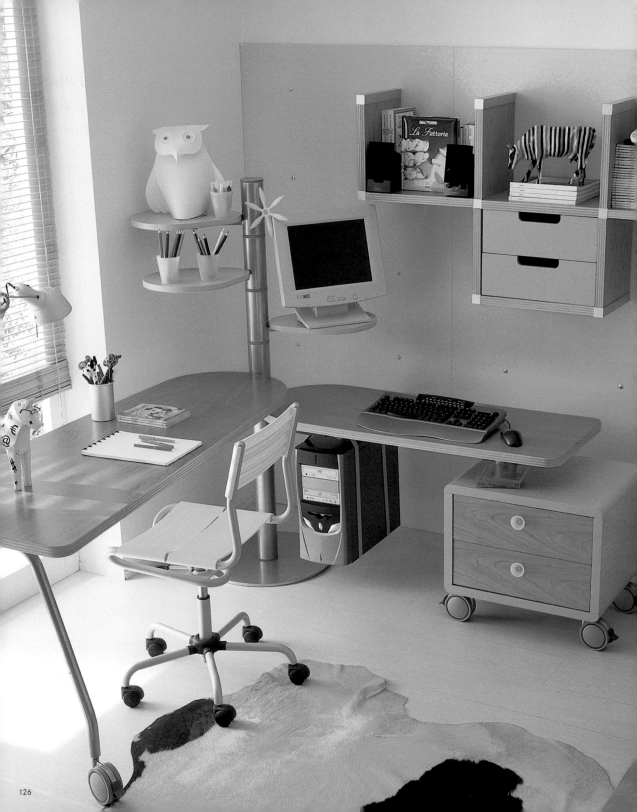

Jungle
Jungle
Dschungel

Dear

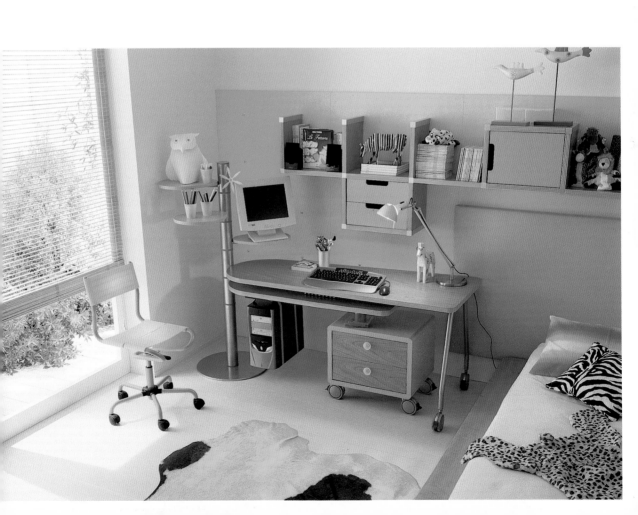

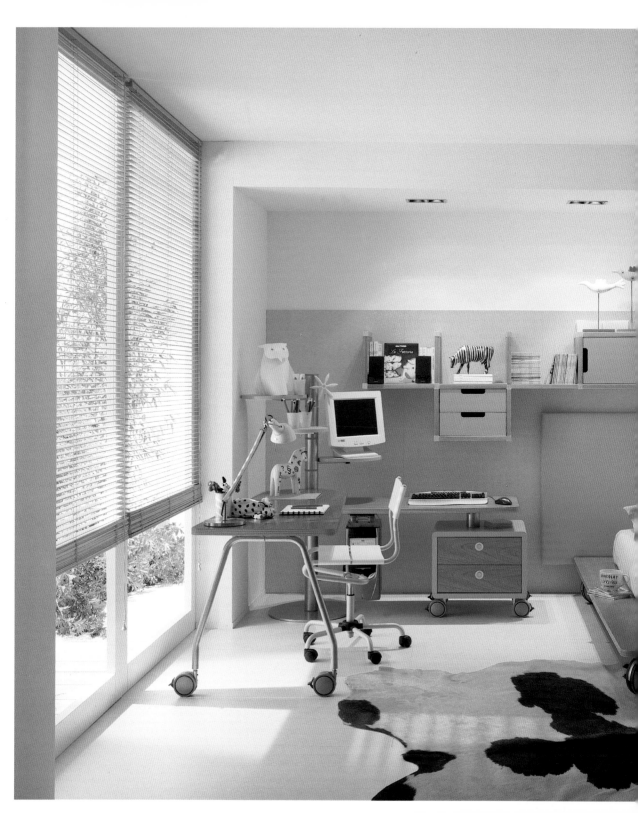

Black Panther

Panthère noire

Schwarzer Panther

Dear

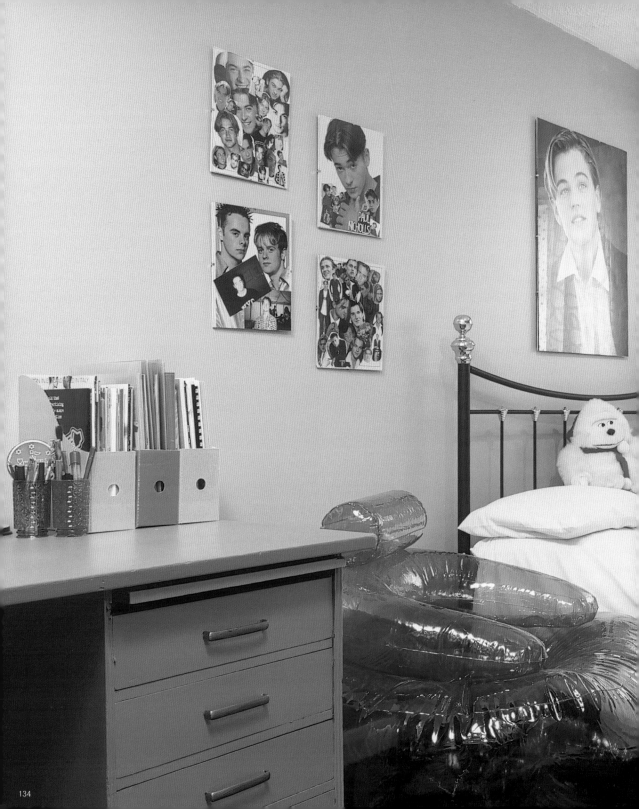

Rascally Animals

Animaux coquins

Freche Tiere

Red
Rouge
Rot
Dear

Sporty Atmosphere
Ambiance sportive
Sportliches Ambiente

Girl's Room
Chambre de fille
Mädchenzimmer

Jenny Norton/Norton Crane

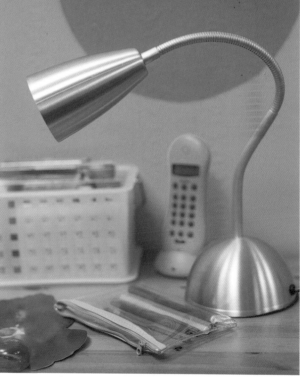

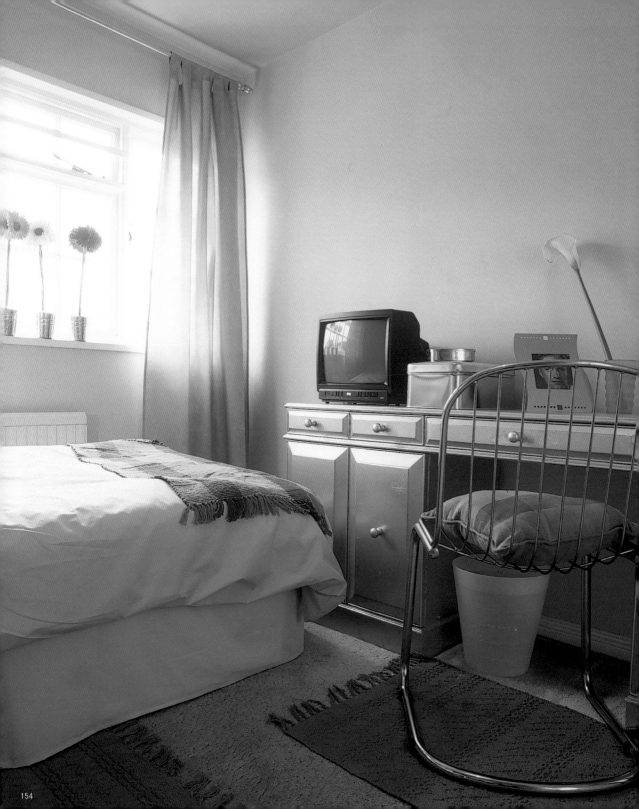

Chill Out

Jenny Norton/Norton Crane

Furniture and Additions
Mobilier et compléments
Mobiliar und Zubehör

When decorating a child's bedroom, it is important to use furniture and accessories that can grow with its ocuppants needs and desires. The basic furniture should be neutral and the accessories should be adaptable to every stage in a child's development. Too much color and infantile design overpowers the space and may not suit the tastes of a teenager. Manufacturers are aware of this factor and offer furniture that can later be enlarged or modified: some cribs, for example, can be converted into couches or even desks.

L'aménagement d'une chambre d'enfant, le mobilier et les accessoires doivent être conçus pour répondre aux besoins et aux désirs de ses petits occupants, et pouvoir évoluer avec eux. L'équipement de base restera plutôt neutre, tandis que les accessoires devront s'adapter aux différents stades du développement de l'enfant. Les excès de couleurs ou un design trop enfantin surchargeant la pièce sont d'ailleurs souvent rejetés par les adolescents. Conscients de ce fait, les fabricants offrent des meubles d'enfants modulables qui peuvent se transformer et s'agrandir au gré des besoins : certains lits de bébés sont convertibles en divans et même en bureau.

Bei der Einrichtung des Kinderzimmers sollten Mobiliar und Zubehör so konzipiert sein, dass sie mit den Anforderungen und Wünschen der Kinder mitwachsen. Deshalb sollte die Grundausstattung eher neutral, die Accessoires hingegen dem jeweiligen Alter angepasst sein. Zu viel Farbe und kindliches Design zum Beispiel überfrachtet nicht nur den Raum, sondern stößt bei Heranwachsenden oft auf Ablehnung. Auch Hersteller haben diesen Gedanken aufgegriffen und bieten Kindermöbel an, die sich umbauen, erweitern und verändern lassen. So gibt es Babybetten, die sich später zur Liege umfunktionieren lassen und bei Bedarf sogar zum Schreibtisch verwandelt werden können.

■ **Furniture**
Meubles
Möbel

■ **Accessories**
Accessoires
Accessoires

■ **Fabrics and Wallpaper**
Tissus et papiers peints
Stoffe und Tapeten

■ **Toys**
Jouets
Spielsachen

Furniture Meubles Möbel

Children's furniture must be very resistant. So, when choosing an item, it is important to consider its resistance and durability, as well as its design. The safety and health of the youngster is paramount. Although furniture that can be easily altered and moved is now fashionable, when there is a shortage of space, bunk beds are ideal for all ages and have retained their classic status.

Les meubles d'enfants doivent être très résistants. Au moment de les choisir, il est essentiel de tenir compte de la sécurité et de la solidité autant que du choix de matériaux ou de l'agencement. Les meubles modulables, faciles à bouger et à transformer, ont le vent en poupe, et les lits superposés, palliant au manque de place, répondent aux critères de toutes les tranches d'âge et restent de grands classiques.

Kinderzimmermöbel müssen viel aushalten, deshalb spielen Sicherheit und Solidität bei der Wahl der Ausstattung, neben gesundheitsverträglichen Materialien und kindgemäßer Gestaltung, eine wichtige Rolle. Flexible Möbel, die sich leicht bewegen und umbauen lassen sind hoch im Trend, während bei Platzmangel Hochbetten den Ansprüchen fast aller Altersklassen gerecht werden und sich als der Klassiker auf dem Markt etabliert haben.

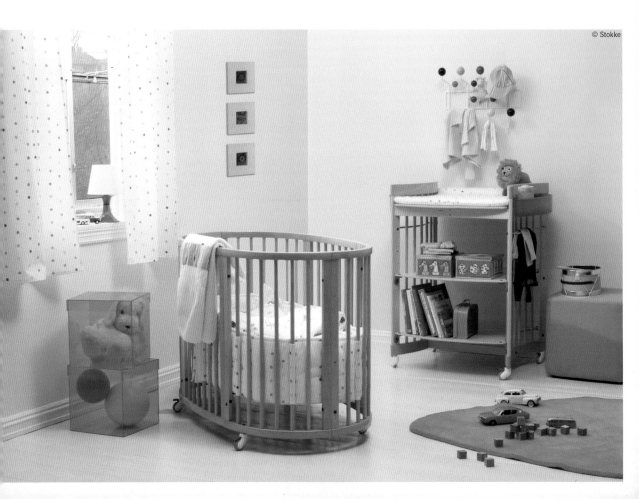

© Stokke

© Bébéform

© MyToys

© Ikea

© Ikea

© Ikea

© MyToys

© Bébéform

© Bébéform

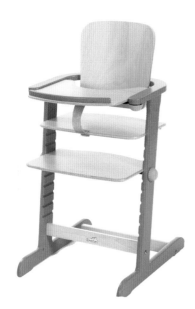

© MyToys

© Marshmallow Company

© Bopita

© Marshmallow Company

© Tarantino Studio

© Live and Play

Accessories Accessoires Accessoires

There are very few limits to the creativity and design of accessories for a child's bedroom, since this is where infantile fantasies and nature are best reflected. Bear-shape lamps, Snow-white mirrors or boxes of toys with lids in the form of turtle bring a child's domain to life, while combining functionality with a design adaptable to any age.

La créativité dans le domaine du design d'accessoires pour chambre d'enfant ne connaît pas de limites, car elle peut refléter la nature et l'imagination de l'enfant. Lampes en forme d'ours, miroirs de Blanche-Neige ou caisses de jouets au couvercle en forme de tortue animent le royaume des enfants en combinant fonctionnalité et design adaptés à chaque tranche d'âge.

Der Kreativität beim Design von Accessoires für Kinderzimmer sind kaum Grenzen gesetzt, da hier die kindliche Natur und Phantasie am besten aufgeriffen und widergespiegelt werden kann. Lampen in Bärenformen, Schneewittchenspiegel oder Spielzeugkisten, die mit einem Deckel in Schildkrötenform verschlossen werden, bringen Leben in das Reich der Kinder und kombinieren Funktionalität mit einem auf jede Altersgruppe zugeschnittenen Design.

© MyToys

© Ikea

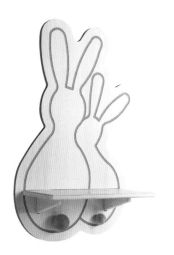

Fabrics and Wallpaper Tissus et papiers peints Stoffe und Tapeten

The choice of fabrics and wallpaper gives a children's room a more personal touch. They can be changed as desired and can even be adapted to the seasons of the year or the required atmosphere, without having to stick to a particular color or style.

Le choix de textiles et de papiers peints permet d'ajouter une touche personnelle à la chambre d'enfant, selon son âge. Ceux-ci sont infiniment variables. Il est possible de les choisir en fonction des saisons ou de l'air du temps sans pour autant trop se résoudre à une couleur ou un style.

Bei der Auswahl von Textilien und Tapeten eröffnet sich die Möglichkeit, dem Kinderzimmer eine auf das jeweilige Alter bezogene, persönliche Note zu verleihen. Dabei lassen sich Textilien wie auch Tapeten beliebig variieren und selbst eine Anpassung an Jahreszeiten oder Stimmungslagen wird möglich, ohne sich jedoch dabei zu stark auf eine Farb- oder Stilrichtung festzulegen.

© Coordonné

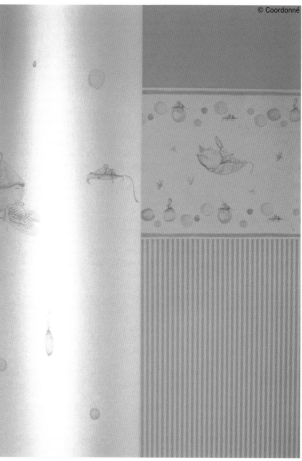

© Coordonné

© Jacadi

© Jacadi

© Tirimilitín

© Tirimilitín

© Tirimilitín

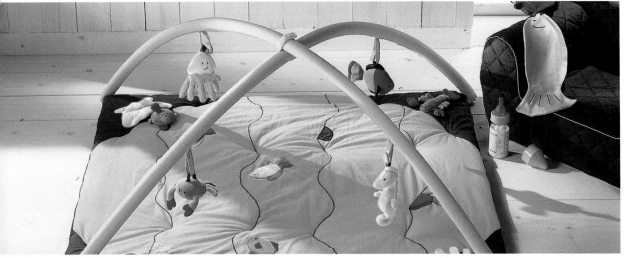

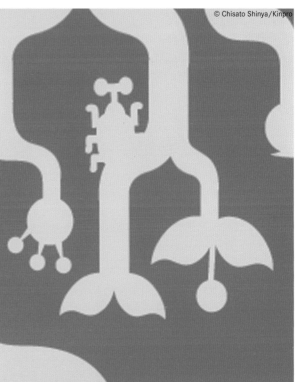

le pt'it JACADI

Toys Jouets Spielsachen

Toys accompany children in their development. Whether soft toys or rocking horses, the variety of designer's ideas combined with the manufacturing possibilities have created very original objects. For example, wooden blocks, as well as stimulating the imagination, are basic for the motor skills development of a child, and also have a decorative function. The selection should meet the safety requirements and also be suited to the particular child's age.

Les jouets accompagnent l'enfant sur le chemin de son développement. Animaux en tissu ou cheval à bascule – l'imagination créatrice des designers, associée aux infinies possibilités de production, façonne les objets les plus originaux. Si les cubes en bois stimulent les mécanismes de la pensée, ils sont également indispensables pour un bon développement moteur, et sont aussi décoratifs. Leur choix se fait en fonction de l'âge et des normes de sécurité.

Spielsachen begleiten Kinder auf ihrem Entwicklungsweg. Ob Stofftiere oder Schaukelpferdchen – der Einfallsreichtum der Designer, kombiniert mit heutigen Herstellungsmöglichkeiten, haben originellste Objekte hervorgebracht. So regen etwa Holzbausteine nicht nur die Denkfunktion an, sie sind auch unerlässlich für eine gesunde, motorische Entwicklung und zudem dekorativ. Die Auswahl sollte dem Alter und den Sicherheitsnormen entsprechen.

© Ikea

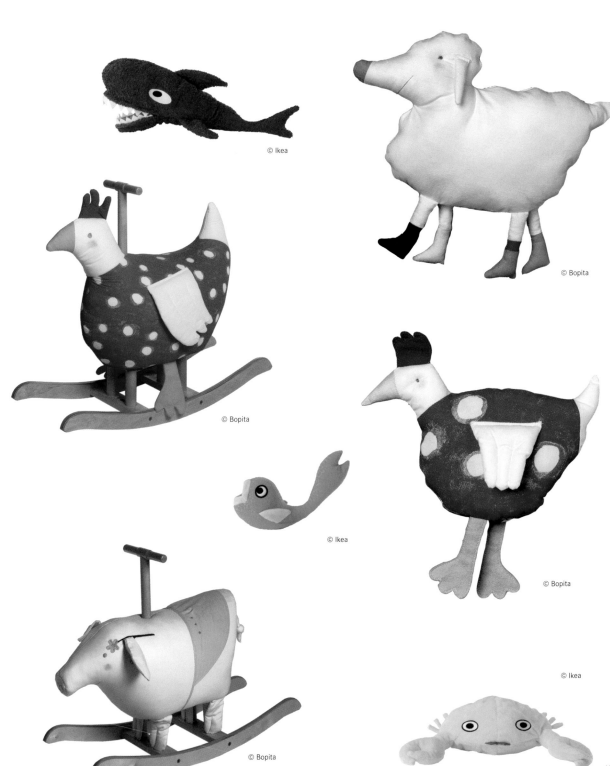

© Ikea

© Bopita

© Bopita

© Bopita

© Ikea

© Bopita

© Ikea

187

Special thanks to Remerciements particuliers à Mit besonderem Dank an

Álex Serra
Amanda Heah/Wigwam Kids
Amelia Aran
Assomobili
Azcue (Design)
Babymobel
BabyRoc/Rocada
Bébéform
Cilek
Dear
Deu i Deu Interiorista/Ana Profitós
Enric Ruiz & Olga Subirós/Cloud 9
Erba Mobili
Estudio Esténcil
Finn & Hattie
Galli
Geuther
Haba
Heather Spencer Designs

Homebase
Ikea
IMA Mobili
Jacadi
Jenny Norton/Norton Crane
Jordi Sarrà
Kinderraeume.com
Leipold
Micuna
Mixel
Mònica Pla
MyJulius/Zöllner
MyToys.de
Patrizia Sbalchiero
Ramón Peñarroya
Tisettanta (Design)
Zalf